Martin Luther King Jr.

Library of Congress Control Number: 2018936551
ISBN 978-1-250-30255-7

Our books may be purchased in bulk for promotional, educational, or business use. Please contact your
local bookseller or the Macmillan Corporate and Premium Sales Department at (800) 221-7945 ext. 5442
or by e-mail at MacmillanSpecialMarkets@macmillan.com.

First published in France in 2016 by Quelle Histoire, Paris
First U.S. edition, 2018

Text: Clémentine V. Baron
Translation: Catherine Nolan
Illustrations: Bruno Wennagel, Mathieu Ferret, Nuno Alves Rodrigues, Claire Martin, Paul Cotoni,
Aurélie Verdon

Printed in China by RR Donnelley Asia Printing Solutions Ltd., Dongguan City, Guangdong Province
10 9 8 7 6 5 4 3 2 1

Martin Luther King Jr.

Roaring Brook Press
New York

Black and White

Martin Luther King Jr. grew up in Atlanta, Georgia. His father was a pastor, and his mother was very involved in their church.

Martin had a friend who lived next door. One day, the boy said he couldn't come to Martin's house anymore. His father wouldn't let him play with a black child. It was the first time Martin felt racism.

As he got older, Martin experienced racism more and more. There were terrible laws in America that kept black people and white people apart, or segregated. Martin made a decision: He wanted to help end those laws.

———

1929

Studies

Martin was a brilliant student. In college, he learned about Gandhi, a spiritual leader in India. Gandhi had made great changes in his country with peaceful protests. Martin thought racist laws could be ended in a peaceful way. But how?

Martin decided to become a pastor. That way he could speak freely and people would hear his ideas.

———

1944

Coretta

In Boston, Martin met a young woman named Coretta Scott. Coretta was studying to be a singer. She was beautiful and talented. She was committed to civil rights, just like Martin. The two fell in love.

Coretta and Martin got married and moved to Montgomery, Alabama, where Martin was going to be the new pastor of a Baptist church.

1952–1954

The Woman Who Said No

Martin hadn't been in Montgomery long when he heard about Rosa Parks. Rosa, a black woman, was riding the city bus one day when the driver told her to give up her seat to a white man. After all, that was the law. "No," said Rosa calmly. The driver called the police. Rosa was taken to jail!

Martin was troubled by Rosa's arrest. He knew other people were, too. He thought it was time for peaceful protest.

———

December 1, 1955

Fighting on Foot

Four days later, Martin gave a fiery sermon. He told his followers to *boycott* the city buses—in other words, to stop riding them. It was a peaceful way to protest how Rosa Parks and all other black riders were being treated.

People listened. African Americans in Montgomery began walking to work even though it took some of them hours.

Weeks passed. The bus companies lost money. Some of them nearly went bankrupt. The boycott was working!

Martin was pleased. People didn't have to fight with their hands, he preached. Instead, they could fight with their heads. Or, in this case, their feet!

———

1955–1956

Dangerous Enemies

Martin received threats because of the boycott. Almost two months after it started, a bomb exploded in his house! Fortunately, no one was hurt.

Martin did not give up. "Hate cannot drive out hate; only love can do that," he said. The boycott kept going. It lasted 381 days!

Finally, the state of Alabama changed its law. Black people no longer had to give up their seats on the bus for white people. For the first time, black and white riders had the same rights!

———

January 30, 1956

"I Have a Dream"

The struggle for equality was far from over.

Martin helped start an organization called the Southern Christian Leadership Conference that set up more peaceful protests. On August 28, 1963, there was a huge march in Washington, DC.

Martin stood before 250,000 people. He gave the most famous speech of his life. "I have a dream," Martin said—a dream of equality and freedom for all humanity.

———

1957–1963

The Civil Rights Act

All the effort paid off. In 1964, President Lyndon B. Johnson signed the Civil Rights Act. The act made it illegal to discriminate against people based on their race, color, religion, sex, or origin. It was a huge victory!

Martin was invited to Norway to receive the Nobel Peace Prize, one of the most important awards in the world. It is given to people who work for peace and justice.

———

1964

Selma

Martin didn't stop. He knew that many African Americans were not allowed to vote, especially in the South. In 1965, Martin set up a big march in Selma, Alabama, to demand voting rights.

Police officers charged into the crowds of protestors. Martin told the marchers to stay peaceful instead of fighting back.

Many protestors were hurt, but the march made a difference. That same year, the Voting Rights Act was passed. Now it was against the law to stop people from voting because of their race.

1965

Tragic End

On April 4, 1968, Martin was shot and killed in Memphis, Tennessee. Many Americans—both black and white—were devastated.

Martin did not end racism in the United States. Sadly, it still exists today. But thanks to brave leaders like him, progress is being made. In 2008, forty years after the death of Martin Luther King Jr., the United States elected its first African American president, Barack Obama. Martin would have been pleased and proud.

———

1968–2008

1920

1929
Martin is born in Atlanta.

1953
Martin marries Coretta Scott.

1954
Martin becomes pastor of the Montgomery Baptist Church.

1955
The Montgo Bus Boyc begins

1951
Martin begins studying theology at Boston University.

1954
Segregation in schools is outlawed. It's no longer legal to have separate schools for black students and white students.

1955
Rosa Parks is arrested for refusing to give up her seat on a bus.

1956
The bus boycott ends after 381 days, and black citizens start riding buses again.

1963
The March on Washington is held. Martin makes his "I Have a Dream" speech.

1964
Martin receives the Nobel Peace Prize.

1968
Martin is assassinated in Memphis, Tennessee.

1970

1956
labama
ges its law,
g black and
e bus riders
ame rights.

1963
There is a major protest against discrimination in Birmingham, Alabama.

1964
President Lyndon B. Johnson signs the Civil Rights Act.

1965
Martin and many others march from Selma to Montgomery for the right to vote.

North America

CANADA

UNITED STATES

Lorraine
MOTEL

MEXICO

2

4

6 5 3 1

MAP KEY

 **Atlanta, Georgia**

The King family's home was located at 501 Auburn Avenue, right next to the church where Martin's father preached. Thousands of people visit it every year.

 **Boston, Massachusetts**

Martin studied theology at Boston University. He also met his wife, Coretta Scott, in Boston.

 **Montgomery, Alabama**

Martin lived in the state capital of Alabama with his family and worked as a pastor. The city is now famous for its role in the civil rights movement.

 **Washington, DC**

On August 28, 1963, approximately 250,000 Americans marched on the streets of Washington to demand equality. Addressing them, Martin delivered his hopeful speech "I Have a Dream."

 **Selma, Alabama**

In March 1965, a big march was organized from Selma to Montgomery to demand that African Americans have the right to vote. It took three tries before marchers reached their destination without being stopped by police.

 **Memphis, Tennessee**

Martin Luther King Jr. was assassinated here, at the Lorraine Motel. A civil rights museum is now housed in this spot.

People to Know

Coretta Scott King
(1927–2006)
Coretta married Martin in 1953. She was his strongest ally and supported him until the end of her life.

Rosa Parks
(1913–2005)
By refusing to give up her seat on the bus, Rosa raised the issue of inequality between black and white citizens. She is called the mother of the civil rights movement.

Lyndon B. Johnson

(1908–1973)

The thirty-sixth president of the United States passed two important laws: the Civil Rights Act in 1964 and the Voting Rights Act in 1965.

Gandhi

(1869–1948)

This Indian spiritual leader was a great source of inspiration for Martin.

....
Martin Luther King Jr. was jailed twenty-nine times during his fight for civil rights.

....
Martin skipped two grades in high school and went to college at the age of fifteen!

Today more than nine hundred streets in the U.S. are named after Martin.

Martin was originally named Michael. His father changed his name to Martin after becoming inspired by Martin Luther, a religious leader from the 1500s.

Available Now

Muhammad Ali

Neil Armstrong

Blackbeard

Coco Chanel

Charlie Chaplin

Cleopatra

Marie Curie

Albert Einstein

Anne Frank

Gandhi

Frida Kahlo

Martin Luther

Abraham Lincoln

Nelson Mandela

Isaac Newton

Rosa Parks

Coming Soon

Marie Antoinette

Buddha

Pocahontas

Vincent van Gogh